James Levi

Refined Not Defined

*God Is Not Defined by Our Circumstances —
We Are Refined Through Them*

James Levi, PhD

Cover design: Lifexcel Publication
Published by: Lifexcel Publication
P.O. Box 953, Huntsville, Texas 77342
**Printed in the United States of America for
worldwide distribution.**

ISBN- 979-8-9922940-0-2

For more information, please contact:
Lifexcel Leadership Publishing
Email: lifexcelleadership@gmail.com

First Edition: 2025

Praise for the book

"James Levi has given the church a gift—an honest, tender, and theologically rich journey into the wilderness places of our lives. *Refined, Not Defined* is a companion for anyone who's ever questioned God in the silence. I found myself seen, strengthened, and ultimately, deeply hopeful."
—**Dr. Bruce Amos**, Pastor and Seminary Professor

"This book is not a manual—it's a mirror. With storytelling, Scripture, and rare vulnerability, James invites us to stop performing and start listening to the God who walks with us in the fire. You won't walk away the same."
—**Jay O'Neal** Christian Author

"James writes like a pastor, thinks like a theologian, and feels like a friend. *Refined, Not Defined* gently dismantles shallow religion and

points us toward a deeper, refining relationship with Jesus. A must-read."
—**Erica Thomas**, Speaker, Mental Health Advocate

"There are books that explain suffering. And there are books that sit with you in it. *Refined, Not Defined* does both. It's raw, real, and redemptive."
—**John Kim**, Lead Pastor, Renew Church

"For anyone who's wondered if they've missed God or fallen too far—this book is your reminder that grace still has the final word. It's wise, warm, and soaked in Scripture."
—**Dr. Melissa Grant**, Author of *Faith After the Fire*

"I wish I had this book ten years ago. James Levi's words gave language to things I've felt but never dared say aloud. This is spiritual formation at its most honest."
—**Nathan Cho**, College Ministry Director, Seattle

Dedication

To you—
standing quietly at your breaking point,
wondering if God still sees,
still cares,
still holds purpose for the pieces of your life.

This book is for you.

May you discover that your circumstances do not
define God—
and that His grace is not absent from the fire,
but *refining you through it.*

And to my two beloved daughters (Saakshi &
Namrata),
walking into your twenties with wisdom and
wonder,
you've taught me more about trust in God than I
could ever teach you.

Your stories remind me—
that God's faithfulness doesn't always feel fast,
but it is always steady.

That His refining is more beautiful than comfort,
more shaping than certainty.

You've shown me that our scars are not signs of
failure,
but places where God's light can shine through.

Thank you for letting me walk beside you,
and for gently helping me believe again—
in grace that transforms,
and love that never lets go.

Foreword

We don't often say it aloud—
but most of us will, at some point,
find ourselves standing in the dark
with a question we don't know how to ask:

"Where is God now?"

It happens after the prayer that didn't get
answered. After the dream that fell apart.
After the grief that didn't go away.
After the silence that stretched too long.

That's the wilderness.

The place where belief gets tested,
where comfort runs out, and where faith is no
longer just something we *know*— it's something
we *fight for.*

Refined, Not Defined was born out of that sacred
terrain—not just as a book,
but as a companion for the days when God feels
silent, and you need to know He's still near.

It's more than a study of Exodus. It's an invitation to walk with Moses, and through him, rediscover a God who doesn't flinch at your breaking point— but draws close in it.

A God who doesn't just deliver you from fire, but meets you *in* it. And refines you *through* it.

"Jesus is not just the one who saves us. He's the one who walks beside us, in sweat, in tears, and in dust."

This journey invites you to hear again— that His promises are louder than the pain. That His love holds even when you let go. That you are not lost in the fire— you are being formed by it.

If you're tired, doubting, grieving, or just hungry for something deeper—you are in the right place.

You are not alone. You are not forgotten. And you are not defined by your past.

Through Christ, you are being refined for something far greater than you can yet see.

Let's walk this journey—together.   – *James Levi*

How to Use This Book

This is not a book to rush through.
It's a book to *walk with*.

To wrestle with.
To weep through.
To sit beside when the night feels long and the answers feel far away.

Every chapter is an invitation:

- To reflect honestly on what hurts, what's broken, and what still lingers.
- To reframe how you see God—not through the lens of pain, but promise.
- To respond—not with perfection, but with presence. With just enough courage to keep going.

At the end of each chapter:

- **Pause at the Reflection Questions.** Let them be your mirror. Journal what rises. That's often where God is already speaking.

- **Pray the Closing Prayer out loud.** Don't recite—*respond.* Let the words become your own cry, your own trust.
- **Connect with someone else.** Healing deepens in shared spaces. Read it with a small group, a friend, or a mentor. Let your wilderness become a shared table.

As you begin:

Be honest. God doesn't need your polished faith—just your open heart.

Be patient. Refinement takes time. Let the fire do its gentle work.

Be prayerful. The Spirit is already shaping you in unseen ways.

Be expectant. Even now, something holy is being born in you.

"I will not leave you as orphans; I will come to you."
—*John 14:18*

The God who walked with Moses walks with you still. The Spirit who raised Christ from the grave is alive in your wilderness.

So open these pages not to finish a book—but to begin a deeper becoming.

You are not defined by your pain.
You are being refined by grace

James Levi

Table of Contents

Listening to God's Heart Over Our Hurt

Even when hope whispers, His voice still speaks louder than your fear.

Trusting Christ to Complete the Work

The fire isn't the end—it's where the gold begins to take shape.

You Are Refined, Not Defined

A benediction for the journey ahead. A whisper that you are not alone.

Keep Walking, Keep Trusting, Keep Becoming

Epigraph

"But He knows the way that I take;

when He has tested me, I will come forth as gold."

— Job 23:10 (NIV)

"God leads every soul by a different path…

but always through fire, silence, and the night.

It is in the dark that we are most deeply refined."

— **St. John of the Cross**

James Levi

Chapter 5: 22 Moses returned to the Lord and said, "Why, Lord, why have you brought trouble on this people? Is this why you sent me? 23 Ever since I went to Pharaoh to speak in your name, he has brought trouble on this people, and you have not rescued your people at all."

Chapter 6: Then the Lord said to Moses, "Now you will see what I will do to Pharaoh: Because of my mighty hand he will let them go; because of my mighty hand he will drive them out of his country."

2 God also said to Moses, "I am the Lord. 3 I appeared to Abraham, to Isaac and to Jacob as God Almighty, but by my name the Lord, I did not make myself fully known to them. 4 I also established my covenant with them to give them the land of Canaan, where they resided as foreigners. 5 Moreover, I have heard the groaning of the Israelites, whom the Egyptians are enslaving, and I have remembered my covenant. 6 "Therefore, say to the Israelites: 'I am the Lord, and I will bring you out from under the yoke of

the Egyptians. I will free you from being slaves to them, and I will redeem you with an outstretched arm and with mighty acts of judgment. 7 I will take you as my own people, and I will be your God. Then you will know that I am the Lord your God, who brought you out from under the yoke of the Egyptians. 8 And I will bring you to the land I swore with uplifted hand to give to Abraham, to Isaac and to Jacob. I will give it to you as a possession. I am the Lord.'"

9 Moses reported this to the Israelites, but they did not listen to him because of their discouragement and harsh labor.

10 Then the Lord said to Moses, 11 "Go, tell Pharaoh king of Egypt to let the Israelites go out of his country."

12 But Moses said to the Lord, "If the Israelites will not listen to me, why would Pharaoh listen to me, since I speak with faltering lips?"

Introduction

When Life Breaks You, What Defines You?

What if the very struggles you're trying to escape

are the places God is trying to refine you?

It's a question we don't like to ask —

until life forces us to.

Eventually, something cracks.

A storm you didn't see coming.

A betrayal that cuts deeper than words.

A dream you carried for years —

now lying in pieces at your feet.

Or maybe it's just the silence.

That long, low ache of waiting…

for healing,

for an answer,

for *something* to change.

And in those moments—

you begin to wonder:

"Where is God now?"

"Has He forgotten me?"

"Does He even care?"

—It's easy to start believing that if life is hard,

God must be distant.

Or worse… indifferent.

Pain starts whispering a new theology:

God only shows up when life works out.

But the Gospel tells another story.

Jesus didn't stay at a distance.

He stepped into our brokenness.

He wore our skin.

Felt our sorrow.

Carried our pain.

Died our death.

And then—

He rose.

—

The Cross doesn't just show us that God cares.

It shows us that He *transforms*.

That suffering in the hands of the Savior

is not wasted.

It's the forge.

Where faith is purified.

Where purpose is uncovered.

Where your identity is no longer what happened

to you,

but what God is doing in you.

—

This book is about *that* refining.

It's about fire that doesn't destroy—

but defines.

A wilderness that doesn't end you—

but frees you.

Through the story of Moses,

and the journey of a wilderness people,

we'll explore how God meets us at our breaking

points:

Not to shame us—

but to reshape us.

Not to crush us—

but to call us deeper.

Not to define us by wounds—

but to refine us in love.

—

Each chapter is a step:

From only seeing the struggle

→ to hearing the promise again.

From wrestling with discouragement

→ to walking in identity.

From doubting His presence

→ to trusting His heart.

—

You are not alone in your questions.

Not abandoned in your pain.

Not defined by your worst day,

your hardest year,

your deepest loss.

Through Christ,

you are being *formed*.

Refined.

Not defined

by the fire you walk through—

but by the God who walks with you.

—

So bring your honest doubts.

Bring your raw prayers.

Bring your fragile faith.

Jesus isn't afraid of your breaking point.

He often does His best work *there*.

Let's begin.

James Levi

Chapter 1

When God Seems Silent

— *Seeing from Our Point of View*

"Why, Lord, why have you brought trouble on this people?" Exodus 5:22–23

Moses did exactly what God told him to do.

He stepped into the calling.

He obeyed.

And everything got worse.

Have you been there?

You finally gather the courage to follow God's
lead—

You pray more earnestly.

You trust harder.

You speak His name out loud…

And somehow, life collapses further.

The silence grows louder.

The suffering intensifies.

And God feels—absent.

That's where Moses was.

After confronting Pharaoh in obedience,

things didn't get better.

The Israelites weren't delivered.

They were punished.

The bricks increased,

but the straw was gone.

And the very people he tried to help turned on

him.

Moses, the once-reluctant messenger,

now stood in the ruins of confusion and

heartbreak.

So he did what we all do when faith collides with

disappointment—

he cried out:

"Why, Lord? Why have you brought trouble on

this people?

Ever since I went to Pharaoh… you have not

rescued your people at all."

(Exodus 5:22–23)

When Faith Feels Like a Setup

Sometimes faith feels like a setup.

You risk—hoping God will meet you halfway—

but the only thing that shows up is more pain.

This wasn't the Moses we met at the burning bush.

This was the Moses after obedience,

after stepping out in trust,

after watching things fall apart anyway.

"God often shows up just after we think He

should have."

— *Frederick Buechner*

A Christmas Story and a Silent Night

It was Christmas.

Cold, ordinary, wrapped in the noise of children

racing around the tree.

The adults gathered around food and

conversation—

a scene that felt predictable, warm, safe.

Then my friend Dave arrived.

His smile was polite, but his eyes were tired.

Later that evening, over coffee, he leaned in and

whispered:

"I just don't feel Him anymore.

I've prayed. I've fasted. I've done everything.

But God is silent.

Like He stepped out of the room and closed the
door behind Him."

I didn't have an answer.
But I knew this moment was holy.

Because it reminded me of *Holy Saturday*—
the day between crucifixion and resurrection.

The day the sky was silent,
the tomb was sealed,
and hope seemed buried.

But it wasn't.
He wasn't.

Jesus was at work in the silence.
And He still is.

"Silence is God's first language. Everything else is a poor translation."

— *St. John of the Cross*

Your Feelings Are Real—But They're Not the Whole Story

What Moses felt was real.

What Dave felt was real.

What you feel is real.

But real doesn't always mean *true*.

Just because God feels absent doesn't mean He is.

Just because we don't hear His voice doesn't mean He's not working.

God's silence is not His absence.

And His delay is not His denial.

Sometimes the silence is the space between the pages.

The pause before the turning of a chapter.

"He is not safe. But He is good."

— *C.S. Lewis, The Lion, the Witch and the Wardrobe*

The Wilderness Is Not Wasted

This part of your life—

the waiting, the disappointment, the ache—

is not a detour.

It's a **refining fire**.

Moses had to unlearn his image of success.

The Israelites had to unlearn their addiction to

immediate answers.

And we?

We're learning that God's love isn't always loud,

or instant,

or easy to feel.

But it is faithful.

"I have learned to kiss the waves that throw me
against the Rock of Ages."

— *Charles Spurgeon*

Transformation doesn't always begin with a
miracle.

Sometimes it begins with a cry in the dark.

A soul whispering,

"Where are You, God?"

and staying there long enough to hear the whisper

back:

"I'm here. Even in this."

Questions for Reflection

- What part of your life feels like God is silent right now?

- Could it be that He is present—just not in the way you expected?

- What might He be forming in you during this season of waiting?

Closing Prayer: *In the Silence, Still*

God,

You feel distant right now.

Quiet.

Still.

I confess—

I've prayed and seen no parting sea,

I've hoped and heard no thunder.

Just stillness.

But maybe,

stillness is not a sign You've left—

but a sign You're inviting me to listen deeper.

So in the waiting,

remind me You are near.

In the silence,

anchor me in trust.

When my eyes can't see,

let my soul remember:

You are not done.

You are still good.

And I am still Yours.

Amen.

James Levi

"God's silence is not His absence—

it's often the space where trust begins to

breathe."

— *from Refined, Not Defined*

James Levi

Chapter 2

Talking to a God Who Is Absent

— *When Silence Doesn't Mean Abandonment*

"Now you will see what I will do..." Exodus 6:1–5

You know the moment.

When your prayers feel like they're bouncing off drywall.

When your worship sounds more like wind in an empty room.

When the ache is real but the answers aren't.

That's where this chapter begins.

With silence.

With confusion.

With the deep, low hum of spiritual fatigue.

It's not that you've lost faith—

you just don't know what to do with it right now.

When Silence Feels Like Abandonment

A friend once told me it felt like God had left the
room

and closed the door behind Him.

I didn't argue.

Because I've felt that too.

There are seasons where even Scripture reads like
static.

Where hope is a memory.

Where joy feels like someone else's story.

That was the world of the Israelites.

Four hundred years of silence.

Four centuries of bricks and backs breaking under

the weight of bondage.

And then—finally—Moses arrives.

He brings fire.

He brings the name of Yahweh.

He brings hope.

But the whip cracks louder.

The bricks pile higher.

And the people begin to wonder:

"Did we make a mistake to believe again?"

"Be patient with the silence of God. He is not ignoring you. He is preparing you."

— *F.B. Meyer*

When Your Instruments Say One Thing

…and Your Gut Says Another

During flight training, I learned to fly through clouds—relying only on instruments.
No horizon. No visual cues. Just trust.

My gut told me we were flying level.
The instruments said we were banking dangerously.
If I trusted my feelings over the gauges, I would crash.

That lesson saved my life.

Because when God feels absent, your emotions scream,

"He's not here. He doesn't care. You're alone."

But Scripture—like cockpit instruments—tells a different story.
It reminds you who God is,
even when the sky is silent and the controls feel loose.

"Never doubt in the dark what God told you in the light."
— *V. Raymond Edman*

Three Moves in the Silence

Moses shows us something profound.

He doesn't fake it.

He doesn't run.

He makes three bold moves that could save your

soul when God feels distant:

1. He Gets Honest

He doesn't sugarcoat his pain.

He doesn't wrap it in spiritual clichés.

He says it plain:

"Why did You even send me?"

"Why have You brought this trouble?"

(Exodus 5:22–23)

This isn't rebellion.

This is relationship.

"Suffering is unbearable if you aren't sure that God is for you and with you."

— *Tim Keller*

Moses wasn't sure about the plan.

But he hadn't let go of the Person.

2. He Speaks Toward, Not Away

Pain wants to make you vent sideways.

Gossip. Withdraw. Rage-scroll your feed.

But Moses? He turns his ache *upward*.

He brings his frustration *to* God—not away from Him.

That's what keeps pain from becoming poison.

That's what transforms despair into prayer.

I remember when one of our daughters was

walking through a season we couldn't fix.

We prayed. We cried. We questioned.

One morning, in a whisper, my wife said:

"Trust—even when you can't see."

And I knew—that wasn't just her voice.

That was God's.

3. He Makes Space to Hear

After pouring it all out, Moses doesn't walk away.

He lingers.

And God responds—not with lightning. Not with

applause.

But with presence.

"I am the Lord.

I have heard.

I remember My covenant.

I will bring you out."

(*Exodus 6:1–5*)

No pep talk.

Just promise.

No explanation.

Just the eternal "I AM."

A Story from the Side of the Road

Bartimaeus. Blind. Forgotten. Left behind.

He sat on the side of the road while the crowd rushed past Jesus.

Everyone else saw a nuisance.

But Bartimaeus saw a chance.

He shouted,

"Son of David, have mercy on me!"

And when they told him to be quiet,

he shouted louder.

And Jesus stopped.

That's what real faith sounds like—

not polished prayers,

but desperate cries that refuse to believe God is too

busy to care.

Jesus walked over.

Saw him.

Healed him.

Loved him.

"God comes to us disguised as our life."

— *Paula D'Arcy*

When the Silence Breaks

When Moses listened—God spoke.

When Bartimaeus cried—Jesus stopped.

And when you keep praying, even when your

heart feels hollow,

you're not being naïve.

You're being brave.

Because the silence is not the end.

It's the stage being set.

"Now you will see what I will do…"

(Exodus 6:1)

This is not the absence.

It's the prelude to breakthrough.

Reflection Questions

- When God seems silent, do you retreat—or cry louder?
- When you feel abandoned, will you speak anyway?
- What if your honesty is the very thing that draws Him near?

Jesus Connection

Jesus is the proof

that God doesn't abandon you in silence—

He enters it.

He was the Word made flesh—

who *became silence* on the cross.

So that in your darkest hour,

you'd never be truly alone.

So keep talking.

Even if your words are just tears.

Even if your prayers feel unanswered.

He's listening.

He always has been.

Even in the silence.

Especially in the silence.

.

Closing Prayer: *When I Can't Feel You*

God,

I can't feel You right now.

Not in the way I used to.

Not in the way I want to.

But I still believe—

even when my voice shakes.

I believe You're not gone.

You're just quiet.

So I won't stop talking.

Even if all I have are sighs and silence.

Even if my prayers feel thin.

Even if the ache speaks louder than my faith.

Remind me of who You are.

Whisper it again—

that You remember,

that You see,

that You're moving even now.

Let Your presence hold what I can't carry.

I will trust,

even in the hush.

Even in the dark.

Amen.

"Silence isn't the absence of God—

it's the pause between the question and the

breakthrough."

—*from Chapter 2, Refined, Not Defined*

James Levi

Chapter 3

From Rescue to Relationship — *Letting God Redefine Our Identity*

"I will redeem you… I will take you as My own people." Exodus 6:6–8

God's goal was never just to get Israel out of Egypt.

His goal was to bring them to Himself.

We want escape.

God offers belonging.

We cry for relief.

God whispers: *I want relationship.*

"God loves each of us as if there were only one of us."
— *St. Augustine*

One of the ways we most often miss God is by being obsessed with what's urgent and obvious... and missing what's eternal and essential.

God sees the whole arc.

We see only the interruption.

We want God to act *now*;

He wants to make us new.

And when He doesn't operate on our timeline,

we feel let down.

Disappointed.

Frustrated.

Or worse—

we start defining Him by our disappointment.

But God isn't on your timeline.

He's on His mission.

And His mission?

Not just to get you out.

But to draw you in.

When the Move Breaks You

We left Utah. The church I loved. The rhythm that
made sense.

I traded meaningful ministry for a mailbox in a
new town that didn't seem to need me.

For months, I wandered.
Prayed.
Knocked.
Nothing.

Until one old man invited me to a prison.

Until a correctional officer mistook me for an
intruder—
and offered me a job.

Until God, in the most unlikely place, whispered
again:
You are not forgotten. You are being refined.

"To the extent that we let go of ourselves, to that extent we are able to receive God."

— *Meister Eckhart*

The Story of the Blacksmith

An old parable tells of a blacksmith who had been through great personal loss.

A friend asked how he could still trust God.

The blacksmith replied:

"When I make a tool, I take the iron and heat it until it's red. Then I strike it with my hammer. If it bends, I know it's becoming strong. But if it breaks, I toss it aside. I don't want to be thrown aside. So I pray: God, strike me if You must—but never throw me away."

God doesn't strike to harm.

He refines to claim.

He wasn't abandoning Israel in their slavery.

He was forming them in the fire.

The Shift in Exodus

Exodus 6:6–8 is more than a promise.

It's a **paradigm shift**:

"I will bring you out…"

"I will rescue you…"

"I will redeem you…"

"I will take you as My own…"

This is not just about **exodus**.

It's about **embrace**.

They had been slaves for generations.

All they knew was *oppression*.

But God was writing a new story—

one where they weren't just freed,

they were *wanted*.

"The desire of God's heart is not just to forgive

you—but to have you."

— *Tim Keller*

God's plan was not to create spiritual escapees.

He was building a people who knew Him.

From **slavery** to **sonship**.

From **trauma** to **truth**.

From **Pharaoh's possession** to **the Father's

embrace**.

Freedom Without Formation?

Freedom without formation leads to wandering.

You can be out of Egypt

but still live like a slave.

Still flinch when things go wrong.

Still react out of fear.

Still wonder if you're loved.

But freedom shaped by relationship—

that's when you stop surviving

and start becoming.

Even Jesus' followers got this wrong.

They thought He came to overthrow Rome.

Instead, He let Rome crucify Him.

They scattered in confusion.

But when He rose,

He didn't appear to the crowds.

He walked a quiet road with two disillusioned disciples.

"Were not our hearts burning within us…?" they later asked (Luke 24:32).

He wasn't rescuing them from pain.

He was walking with them through it—

and revealing Himself.

God's Invitation

"I will take you as My own people."

That's the heart of God.

You are not just someone He helps.

You are someone He *chooses*.

- From **oppression** to **intimacy**

- From **rescue** to **relationship**

- From **broken identity** to **beloved identity**

"The deepest truth about you is not what you feel,

not what others say, and not what you've done.

It is what God says about you: You are mine."

— *Henri Nouwen*

Reflection

Are you just asking God to change your
circumstance—
or are you open to letting Him change *you*?

Are you seeking a fix—
or an encounter?

Because relationship is where identity gets
redefined.

And identity is what sustains you
when rescue doesn't come
as quickly
as you hoped.

Jesus Connection

Jesus didn't die to make you a spiritual refugee.

He died to make you family.

The Cross isn't a life hack.

It's a homecoming.

You're not just *saved*.

You're *known*.

Not just *forgiven*.

Adopted.

Not just *set free*.

Set apart.

You belong.

Closing Prayer: *Belonging Before Doing*

God of rescue and relationship,

I come to You not just with my needs,

but with my need *for You*.

I confess I often want You to fix my situation

more than I want to be formed by You.

But today… I pause.

I listen.

I open my clenched hands.

You are not just the One who brings me out—

You are the One who brings me close.

So take me as Your own.

Not because I've earned it,

but because You've chosen me.

Write Your name over my story.

Define me by Your love—

not by what I've lost,

not by what I fear,

not by the chains I still carry in my mind.

Teach me to live

as someone who *belongs*.

Amen.

Guided Reflection

Take a few quiet moments. Breathe deeply.

Ask yourself—

"Where in my life am I waiting for rescue,

but missing the invitation to relationship?"

Then ask—

"If I believed I truly belonged to God…

how would I live differently today?"

Let that question stay with you.

Don't rush it.

Let it speak to your heart.

James Levi

"You are not just freed from something—

you are being drawn into Someone."

— from Chapter 3, Refined, Not Defined

James Levi

Chapter 4

When Discouragement Drowns Hope —

Listening to God's Heart Over Our Hurt

"But they did not listen to him because of their discouragement and harsh labor." Exodus 6:9–12

Sometimes the promises of God fall on deaf ears—

not because He's gone silent,

but because we're drowning in sorrow.

This was Israel's reality.

The pain was louder than the promise.

The bruises on their backs spoke louder than the words from Moses' mouth.

Their trust had been fractured.

Their faith—fragile.

Even Moses, God's mouthpiece, cracked under the weight:

"If the Israelites won't listen to me, why would Pharaoh?"

This is what discouragement does.

It deafens you.

Not just to people—

but to God.

But God keeps speaking.

Even when no one's listening.

Even when hearts are hard, and hope is fading.

He keeps whispering—because He's not just trying to deliver us.

He's trying to *define* us.

The Fragile Thread of Hope

Hope is the oxygen of the soul.

Without it, we suffocate in despair.

Without hope, we stop dreaming.

We stop believing that redemption is possible.

"Hope has two beautiful daughters:

their names are Anger and Courage.

Anger at the way things are,

and Courage to see that they do not remain as they are."

— *St. Augustine*

But hope is delicate.

It bruises easily in harsh conditions.

And when we lose it,

we don't just doubt ourselves—

we start doubting *God*.

We begin to wonder if He's still good,

or if He's even *there*.

And when hope breaks down, so does the refining

process.

No hope—no healing.

No hope—no forward movement.

The tragedy?

We often settle for false hope instead—

hope that makes us comfortable, not whole.

1. Why Hope Matters

Exodus 6 is God stepping into the story again.

He's not quiet.

He's not distant.

He shows up with a promise:

"I am the LORD… I will bring you out… I will redeem you… I will take you as My own."

But they couldn't hear Him.

"They did not listen to him because of their discouragement and harsh labor."

Trauma turns down the volume of God's voice and amplifies the voice of pain.

Sometimes we don't reject God's promise because
we don't believe it—
we just can't *bear* to believe it.

Because if we let ourselves hope, and it doesn't
happen,
we fear the disappointment will destroy us.

So we guard our hearts by going numb.

But God doesn't call you to protect your heart
with fear.
He calls you to anchor your heart in hope.

"The cross shows us that suffering and love are not
opposites.
The place of pain may also be the place of
presence."
— *Fleming Rutledge*

2. Why Hope Gets Lost

a. When God doesn't meet our expectations.

The Israelites expected immediate deliverance.

Instead, Pharaoh doubled their workload.

So they stopped trusting.

Stopped listening.

Stopped hoping.

This happens to us, too.

We expect God to move by Friday.

When He doesn't, we assume He's not moving at

all.

But God is not bound by our urgency.

He's working at the level of *eternity*.

b. When our identity is shaped by oppression.

Pharaoh's real power wasn't just in his armies—

it was in his *words*.

"They will rise up."

"They must be controlled."

"They are a threat."

He built policy on fear.

And Israel began to believe it.

They forgot their story.

Forgot the God of Abraham, Isaac, and Jacob.

Forgot Joseph.

Forgot the promise.

Oppression doesn't just steal your freedom—

it rewrites your memory.

You forget who you are.

You forget you were made for something more.

And when you forget who you are,

you stop looking for deliverance.

You just try to survive.

"Despair is the absolute extreme of self-love.

It is reached when a man deliberately turns his

back on all help from others."

— *Thomas Merton*

3. False Hope vs. True Hope

Pharaoh offered just enough to survive—

but never enough to be free.

That's what false hope does.

It soothes you in slavery.

It teaches you to call your chains *normal*.

True hope?

True hope breaks chains.

False hope says: *This is all there is.*

True hope says: *God is not done yet.*

"Christian hope is not the same as optimism.
It is not the conviction that something will turn
out well,
but the certainty that something makes sense,
regardless of how it turns out."
— *Václav Havel*

Gospel Parallel: Jairus and His Daughter

In Mark 5, Jairus pleads with Jesus:
"My daughter is dying. Come quickly."

Jesus agrees—but pauses to heal a woman along
the way.
Delay.

Then the news:

"Your daughter is dead."

Hope, gone.

But Jesus turns to Jairus and says:

"Don't be afraid. Just believe."

Translation:

Don't let the delay cancel your faith.

Don't let the timeline define the outcome.

Jesus enters the house.

Takes her by the hand.

And says:

"Little girl, I say to you, get up."

She rises.

Because when Jesus is present,

hope is never truly dead.

The Story of the Ember

In a forest after wildfire,

a park ranger once spotted something strange.

Charred ground, smoke rising…

but in the ashes, a single ember glowed.

Faint. Fragile. But still alive.

They gently cupped it, fanned it, protected it.

And in time, it sparked a flame again.

This is what God does with our hope.

Even if it's only an ember,

He doesn't extinguish it.

He fans it back into fire.

"A bruised reed He will not break,

and a smoldering wick He will not snuff out."

— *Isaiah 42:3*

God's Invitation to You

God is not asking you to pretend.

He knows the hurt is real.

But He's asking you not to let the *hurt* define what

is *possible*.

He's still speaking.

Still refining.

Still calling.

And He wants to pull you out of the despair

that tells you this is all there will ever be.

This is not the end of your story.

It's the place where God does His deepest work.

Reflection

- What pain has drowned out the promises of God in your life?
- Have you mistaken God's delay for His denial?
- What ember of hope still remains— however faint?

Jesus Connection

Jesus is still speaking—

even if your heart is too tired to hear.

His voice is not demanding.

It's gentle. Healing. Restoring.

He comes into your hopeless places

not with pressure—

but with presence.

And when He speaks,

even what was dead

can rise again.

Closing Prayer: *When Hope Feels Fragile*

God of the Ember,

You see me when my faith is tired

and my heart is overwhelmed.

You know the weight I carry—

the voices that have grown louder than Yours,

the delays that have tested my trust,

the silence that has felt like absence.

But You are still here.

You are not impatient with my weakness.

You are not threatened by my doubt.

You speak gently to me,

even when I struggle to listen.

So here I am—

with my bruised hope,

my tired soul,

my smoldering faith.

Fan it back into flame.

Whisper louder than the lies.

Lift my head above the noise.

Let me hear Your heart again—

the one that still calls me chosen,

loved,

held. Amen.

"Even when hope feels like a dying ember—
God is not finished. *His voice still speaks life into
what feels lost.*"

— *from Chapter 4, Refined, Not Defined*

James Levi

Chapter 5

Seeing God's Point at Our Breaking Point — *Trusting Christ to Complete the Work*

"I am the Lord... I will bring you out... I will redeem you... I will take you as my own people." Exodus 6:6–7

At some point, we all arrive there.

The edge.

The end.

The place where your prayers feel unanswered, where the pain outpaces the promises, and all that once felt certain now feels impossibly distant.

The *breaking point*.

"The Lord allows the soul to be brought to the edge—

not to destroy her, but to awaken her."
— *St. Teresa of Ávila*

This chapter brings us to the crossroads:
Will we be **defined** by our pain—
or **refined** by His promises?

Everything we've walked through in the past chapters—
pain, silence, discouragement, identity—
converges here.

Because the breaking point is not the end.

It's the invitation.

1. Remembering the Journey

Let's pause and look back:

- We've named the silence.

- Faced the discouragement.

- Wrestled with the lies.

- Rediscovered our identity.

- And caught glimpses of God in the fire.

Now the question is not *"Does God see me?"*

but *"Do I still trust what He already said?"*

"What is true in the light must remain true in the dark."

— *Corrie ten Boom*

2. Hearing Hope Through the Noise

God's help often comes wrapped in weakness.

Moses was no charismatic leader.

He was a fugitive with a speech impediment.

But he had heard God.

And now, he carried a promise.

"I am the Lord… I will redeem you…"

But the people couldn't hear it.

Because the noise of oppression was louder than

the whisper of hope.

That's what happens at the breaking point:

God speaks, but pain shouts.

Yet the chains didn't start breaking when Pharaoh

gave in.

They began to break

when the people began to *see* again—

to listen,

to believe,

to remember who they were

and whose they were.

"Faith is the bird that feels the light and sings

while the dawn is still dark."

— *Rabindranath Tagore*

3. His View vs. Ours

Let's be honest—our view is small.

We see moments.

God sees generations.

We react to pressure.

God responds with purpose.

In Exodus 6, God doesn't begin with solutions—
He begins with **identity**.

"I am the Lord… I have remembered My
covenant…"

This is not improvisation.
This is fulfillment.
Before the Israelites were slaves,
they were *chosen*.

And the same is true of you.

Our View:

- I feel forgotten.

- My identity is broken.

- My strength is gone.

God's View:

- I have remembered you.

- You are My beloved.

- I will carry you.

"God's promises are not fragile. They are forged in eternity."
— *Tim Keller*

4. When Promises Seem Distant

Let me tell you a story.

There was a woman—a friend of our family.
Raised in faith.
Raised on promises.
And for a while, it seemed like they were all coming true.

She married a man who talked the talk,

who knew the language of faith,

but who never let God into the broken parts.

He had learned religion.

But he hadn't learned healing.

When the pressures of life came,

he turned to control.

To shame.

To silence.

And she—once vibrant and full of hope—began to

shrink.

She started believing the pain.

She started redefining God through the wounds.

Until one morning,

when her soul had reached its breaking point,

a whisper broke through.

A memory. A phrase.

A voice deep within:

"You are still Mine."

That voice didn't remove the pain immediately.

But it reoriented everything.

She chose to believe again—

not in the situation,

but in the **God beyond it**.

And healing followed.

5. God's Promises Precede Our Pain

That's the beauty of Exodus 6.

Before the first plague,

before the first miracle,

before Pharaoh even blinked—

God had already spoken.

"I will bring you out…"

"I will redeem you…"

"I will take you as My own…"

Deliverance wasn't plan B.

It was always the plan.

And the same is true for you.

The promise came before the problem.

And it will still stand

when the pain is gone.

"The devil may build his furnaces hot, but God keeps His hand on the thermostat."

— *Charles Spurgeon*

6. Let Hope Lead You Out

At your breaking point, everything in you will want to run—

from people,

from God,

from yourself.

But don't run.

Pause.

Listen again.

Because sometimes

God's greatest work begins

at the moment you thought it was over.

"It is not that we find hope. It's that hope finds

us—

when we are still enough to hear it."

— *Henri Nouwen*

7. Jesus, the Better Moses

Jesus doesn't just speak hope—

He *is* hope.

He doesn't come to offer escape.

He comes to offer **transformation**.

The Cross was His breaking point.

And yet—

from that place of suffering,

He accomplished salvation.

"What was meant to crush Him became the foundation of our redemption."

— *N.T. Wright*

When You Trust Jesus—The Refiner

- Your breaking point becomes a **birthing place**.
- Your identity is **restored**.
- Your story is **rewritten**.
- And your hope leads you **forward**.

Reflection

- Are you defining God through your pain—
or letting Him redefine you through His
promise?
- Is there a voice of hope God is sending that
you've been too tired to hear?
- What part of your story needs to be seen
through *God's* point of view?

Jesus Connection

The Cross looked like the end.
But it became the beginning.

Trust the One who sees you,
knows you,

and has already spoken

a better word over your life.

He's not improvising your redemption.

He's completing it.

.

Closing Prayer: *The Work You Began*

Jesus,

You see the cracks in me—

the places where hope has leaked,

where promises feel distant,

where the weight of pain feels heavier than Your

Word.

But today, I choose to believe again.

I trust that You are not finished.

That what You began in me,

You will carry to completion.

Help me stop defining You by what hurts,

and start seeing You in what heals.

Let Your promise speak louder than the pressure.

Let Your voice rise above the noise.

And let Your Spirit complete in me

what I could never finish on my own.

I am Yours.

Even here.

Especially here.

Amen.

James Levi

"The breaking point is not where your story ends— it's where the promise begins to rise."

—*from Chapter 5, Refined, Not Defined*

James Levi

120

Final Reflection

Will You Let Christ Refine You — *or Let Pain Redefine You?*

When the mountains feel immovable,

When prayers go unanswered,

When hope slips through your fingers—

This is the moment when everything seems to fall apart.

But maybe, just maybe, it's the place where everything begins.

I began this journey in the pages of Exodus.

What started as a Bible study became a lifeline—

not just for those I serve, but for my own soul.

The wilderness spoke.

The silence echoed.

The pain revealed what theology often hides.

And what I found there—

was a God not absent from suffering,

but present within it.

A God not shaped by pain,

but one who steps into it

to shape us.

"God whispers to us in our pleasures, speaks in our consciences,

but shouts in our pains: it is His megaphone to rouse a deaf world."

— *C.S. Lewis*

This book was written for those who feel like they're walking through fire.

Not just because life is hard—

but because faith feels fragile.

God feels distant.

And you're not sure what you believe anymore.

If that's you,

you're not alone.

And you're not broken beyond repair.

You may have been taught a version of God

formed more by fear than by faith.

A God who punishes quickly, forgives reluctantly,

and avoids the hurting.

But that's not Jesus.

Jesus doesn't flinch at your breaking point.

He walks straight into it.

"We can only be said to be alive in those moments when our hearts are conscious of our treasures."
— *Thornton Wilder*

A Story: The Fire That Made Her

A friend once told me about her grandmother—
a quiet, faithful woman who had survived the Partition of India.
She lost her parents, her siblings, everything she knew—
forced to flee with nothing but the clothes on her back and a small, handwritten psalm folded in her blouse.

For years she spoke little of it.
But every morning, without fail, she read that psalm.

And one day, when asked why she didn't give up on God, she replied:

"I didn't read those words to remember a God who *rescued* me.

I read them to remember a God who *stayed*."

Even when she couldn't feel Him.

Even when the story didn't make sense.

She believed the story wasn't over.

And that made all the difference.

"All the darkness in the world cannot extinguish the light of a single candle."

— *St. Francis of Assisi*

Your Crossroads

We all have a choice in our pain.

Moses had his—burning bush, broken heart,

faltering lips.

And he turned aside to see.

That decision changed the course of history.

You have yours.

You can define God by what happened to you.

Or you can let God *refine* you through what

happened.

Pain doesn't get the last word.

Christ does.

"The soul is like a window through which God's

light enters.

When it is clean and transparent, it shines

brightly;

when covered in dust and cracks, it still holds the

light, but it needs healing."

— *St. John Climacus*

The God Who Steps In

The God of the Bible does not live far away.

He stepped into the cries of slaves in Egypt.

He knelt in the garden under the weight of

sorrow.

He stretched out His hands on a cross—

and shattered the silence with resurrection.

"He did not come to explain away suffering,

but to fill it with His presence."

— *Paul Claudel*

He's not watching from a distance.

He's closer than the ache.

And more faithful than the pain.

Remember This:

- God is not defined by your circumstances.

- You are being refined through His love.

- You are not alone in the fire.

- You are not what happened to you.

- You are who God is shaping you to become.

Choose Today:

- Trust His **character** over your emotions.

- Let His **Spirit** rewrite your vision.

- Follow His **voice**, even when it whispers.

- Don't walk away.

- Walk toward Him.

"He who began a good work in you will carry it on to completion until the day of Christ Jesus."

— *Philippians 1:6*

Closing Prayer

Jesus,

When I can't see the path,

help me to trust Your heart.

When I don't feel Your presence,

remind me that You're still holding me.

When I am at the end of myself,

let that be the place You begin again.

Refine what is broken.

Redeem what was lost.

Resurrect what feels dead.

I want to see You—not through the lens of my

hurt,

but through the power of Your promise.

Take all that I am.

All that I fear.

All that I hope for.

And shape it

into something eternal.

Amen.

James Levi

"You are not defined by what you've been through—You are being refined by the One who walked through it with you."

— *from Refined, Not Defined*

James Levi

Benediction: *To the One Being Refined*

May you walk forward

not with answers—

but with **presence**.

Not with control—

but with **trust**.

When the fire comes,

may you remember it does not consume—

it purifies.

When the silence lingers,

may you hear the whisper that never left.

When the pain feels like too much,

may you know

you are being held

by the One who bore it all.

Go now,

refined—not defined—

by grace.

Go now,

as one who belongs

to the Light that will never be overcome.

Amen.

Next Steps

Keep Walking. Keep Trusting. Keep Becoming.

Finishing a book like this isn't the end.

It's the **turning of a page**,

the beginning of a new chapter—

not just in your story,

but in your **becoming**.

Because the goal of this journey isn't to feel better.

It's to be **made new**.

You are not too broken.

You are not too far gone.

And you are not alone.

"The glory of God is man fully alive."

— *St. Irenaeus*

1. Return Daily to God's Word

Let His words be louder than your wounds.

Scripture isn't just for study—it's for **strength**.

- When weary: turn to the *Psalms* and sit in them.
- When confused: revisit *Exodus 3–6* and remember the God who shows up in burning bushes.
- When longing for hope: soak in *Romans 8* or *2 Corinthians 4*.

Let the Word reshape your narrative.

"Let the Bible be the compass, not the mirror. It doesn't show you how you feel—it shows you where to go."

— *Tim Keller*

2. Stay in Honest Conversation with God

Prayer isn't performance.

It's presence.

You don't need eloquence.

You need honesty.

- Tell Him the truth: "God, I'm tired." "God, I'm angry." "God, I want to trust again."
- Keep a journal. Not for answers, but for clarity.
- Let your prayers be as messy as your story.

"O Lord, make me want what you already want to give."

— *St. Augustine*

3. Surround Yourself with the Right People

God often speaks through others.

He heals in the context of community.

- Find people who speak hope when you forget how.

- Lean into mentors who remind you of who you are.

- Don't wait until you feel strong. Reach out while still trembling.

"What we cannot carry alone, we carry together. And it becomes light."

— *Dietrich Bonhoeffer*

4. Reflect—Don't Run

Pain that is buried becomes pain that controls. But pain that is **brought to God** becomes part of your redemption.

- Ask: "How has this pain shaped how I see God?"
- "What is God trying to say to me through this?"
- "Where might trust begin again?"

5. Make a Simple Declaration

This one sentence may become the foundation of your next season:

"I will not be defined by what happened to me. I will be refined by what God is doing in me."

Write it. Say it.

Pray it until it begins to shape your lens.

A Short Story: The Fire That Brought Her Home

A young artist I once knew spent years perfecting

her work—

but when her fiancé walked away just weeks

before their wedding,

her entire world shattered.

The confidence she had in herself,

in love,

in God—collapsed.

She stopped painting. She stopped praying.

She stopped believing.

Until one day, she visited an exhibit

on **Kintsugi**—the Japanese art of mending broken

pottery with gold.

Instead of hiding the cracks, the artists filled them with shimmering seams.

She stared at one bowl for a long time.

Then whispered to herself:

"Maybe my scars can be seen too. Maybe they don't ruin the story—they *make* it."

That week, she picked up her brushes again.

Her next piece?

A portrait of a broken vessel—

lined with gold.

"God is the one who turns wounds into windows and cracks into channels of light."

— *Ann Voskamp*

Daily Declaration

Speak this over your life each morning:

Today, I choose not to be defined by my pain.

I am being refined by the love and truth of Jesus.

I reject the lie that my circumstances have the final word.

I embrace the promise that God is not finished with me.

I am not a mistake. I am not forgotten.

I am a child of God—seen, loved, and called.

Christ is with me in the fire.

His Spirit is shaping me into who I was always meant to be.

I will walk by faith, not by fear.

I will trust the Refiner—today and every day.

Guided Journal Prompts

Let these prompts guide your healing.

You don't need to finish them all—just begin.

Let the process be slow, sacred, and safe.

Identity

- What lies have I believed about myself because of pain or failure?

- What truth does God speak over me in Scripture?

- Where do I need to release shame and receive grace?

God's Character

- Have I defined God through my circumstances or His covenant?

- What part of God's heart do I need to rediscover?
- What promise do I need to hold onto right now?

Hope and Healing

- What has been stealing my hope?
- When did I last feel peace? What made it possible?
- How might God be inviting me to trust again?

Refinement

- Where do I feel stretched or stripped?
- What might God be shaping in this season?
- Who am I becoming through this fire?

Moving Forward

- What is one step of obedience I can take this week?
- Who can walk beside me in this?
- What does it look like to live "refined, not defined" in my daily life?

"Start where you are. Use what you have. Trust who He is."

— *Unknown*

REMEMBER THIS

"You are not defined by what you've been through—
You are being refined by the One who walked through it with you."

Visit: <u>www.jameslevi.org</u> for more tools, teachings, and encouragement.

Chapter Reflection Guide

A space to reflect, to remember, to return.

Chapter 1 — When God Seems Silent

"Why, Lord?" — Exodus 5:22

- What recent moment left you breathless with disappointment or aching with unanswered questions?

- In that moment, where did your soul turn?

  - Did you walk away in frustration?

  - Retreat into numbness or routine religion?

o   Or did you, even faintly, lean toward Jesus—just enough to whisper a prayer?

Chapter 2 — Talking to a God Who Is Absent

"Now you will see what I will do." — Exodus 6:1

- Where in your life are you struggling to believe that God sees you?
- What promise feels distant—but still faintly familiar?
- How can remembering the Cross—where silence met salvation—anchor your trust again?

Chapter 3 — From Rescue to Relationship

"I will take you as My own people." — *Exodus 6:7*

- Are you seeking God as a means of escape—or as the One you long to know, even in the storm?

- What would it look like to stop asking only for relief… and start asking for *relationship*?

Chapter 4 — When Discouragement Drowns Hope

"But they did not listen because of their discouragement." — *Exodus 6:9*

- What part of your life has been silenced by discouragement?

- Where have you stopped dreaming?

- Is there a whisper—soft, persistent—calling your name again?

What would it take to sit still long enough to hear Jesus say, *"Don't be afraid. Just believe."*?

Chapter 5 — Seeing God's Point at Our Breaking Point

"I am the Lord… I will redeem you." — Exodus 6:6

- What would it look like for you to trust Jesus *here*—

  not just to rescue you,

  but to refine you?

- How is He inviting you to stop defining your life by what broke you…

  and start being reshaped by the One who walks with you through the fire?

"You are not who the pain says you are.

You are who God is forming you to become."

— *from Refined, Not Defined*

James Levi

Scripture Reference List

Chapter 1: When God Seems Silent — *Trusting Beyond the Pain*

- Exodus 5:22–23
- Psalm 22:1
- John 14:18
- Luke 24:13–35

Chapter 2: Talking to a God Who Feels Absent

- Exodus 6:1–5
- Psalm 13:1–2
- John 11:21–26
- Romans 8:24–25

Chapter 3: From Rescue to Relationship

- Exodus 6:6–8
- Romans 8:15–17
- John 15:15
- Luke 24:30–32

Chapter 4: When Discouragement Drowns Hope

- Exodus 6:9–12
- Mark 5:35–42
- Psalm 42:5
- Isaiah 43:1–2

Chapter 5: Seeing God's Point at Our Breaking Point

- Exodus 6
- Romans 5:3–5
- 2 Corinthians 4:16–18
- John 1:5
- Mark 5:36

Reference List

The following is a consolidated list of all non-biblical sources quoted or referenced throughout this book.

Bell, Rob. *What We Talk About When We Talk About God*. New York: HarperOne, 2013.

Comer, John Mark. *The Ruthless Elimination of Hurry*. Colorado Springs: WaterBrook, 2019.

Hurnard, Hannah. *Hinds' Feet on High Places*. Carol Stream, IL: Tyndale House Publishers, 1975.

Keller, Timothy. *Walking with God through Pain and Suffering*. New York: Penguin Books, 2013.

Lewis, C.S. *A Grief Observed*. San Francisco: HarperOne, 2001.

Scazzero, Peter. *Emotionally Healthy Spirituality: It's Impossible to Be Spiritually Mature While Remaining Emotionally Immature*. Grand Rapids: Zondervan, 2006.

Willard, Dallas. *The Divine Conspiracy: Rediscovering Our Hidden Life in God*. New York: HarperOne, 1998.

Wright, N.T. *Surprised by Hope: Rethinking Heaven, the Resurrection, and the Mission of the Church*. New York: HarperOne, 2008.

James Levi

About the Author

James Levi, Ph.D. is a pastor, retreat speaker, and storyteller—
but more than that, he is a fellow traveler through the wilderness of faith.

His life's work—through teaching, writing, and mentoring—has been to help others rediscover a God who doesn't stand at a distance, but enters the silence, walks through the fire, and gently reshapes our stories from the inside out.

James is the author of ten books, including *The Light Maker*—a luminous call to live with identity, purpose, and courage in a world searching for meaning. His words are more than chapters on a page; they're invitations. Invitations to grieve honestly, hope defiantly, and believe deeply in a love that refines, not defines.

Whether in the pulpit or at the page, he carries a single desire:

To help you see that your life—especially the broken parts—is not a detour.
It's the sacred ground where transformation begins.

When he's not writing or speaking, James is usually in the sky as a licensed pilot, or at a kitchen table—sharing coffee, listening deeply, and reminding others (and himself) that grace is still enough.

Back Cover

When life breaks you, who gets the final word—your pain or your God?

You prayed.
You hoped.
And still, the silence lingered.
The mountain didn't move.
The story didn't go the way you thought it would.

But what if your breaking point
isn't where it ends—
it's where something holy begins?

In *Refined, Not Defined*, James Levi guides you
through the raw beauty of Exodus 5–6, offering a
fresh invitation:
To stop letting pain tell your story.
And start letting God rewrite it.

This is not about escaping the fire.
It's about meeting the Refiner in it.

Inside these pages, you'll rediscover a God who
doesn't just rescue you from hardship —

He steps into it,
walks with you through it,
and uses it to shape you
into who you were always meant to become.

You are not too broken.
You are not too far gone.
You are not forgotten.

You are being refined.
Not defined.
And your story is not over.